Published in 1993 by
Troddy Books
An imprint of
Regency House Publishing Limited
The Grange
Grange Yard
London SE1 3AG

ISBN 1 85361 356 8

Printed in Italy.

My First Learning Series
TIME

Written and Illustrated by
Caroline and John Astrop

TRODDY BOOKS

7 o'clock
Ted quickly jumps out of bed.
Do you get up at 7 o'clock?

Which animals are quick and which are slow?

8 o'clock
Ted has porridge for breakfast.
What do you like for breakfast?

Find the right breakfast for each friend.

9 o'clock
Ted rides his tricycle.
How many flowers can you see?

10 o'clock
Time to tidy Ted's room.
Is your room tidy?

11 o'clock
Ted helps dad in the garden.
What is Ted doing?

Help Sam snail find his way out of the garden.

12 o'clock
Ted has lunch with the toys.
What do you think these toys are called?

1 o'clock
Tired Ted takes a nap.
Who else is asleep?

2 o'clock
Time to play.
How many friends has Ted?

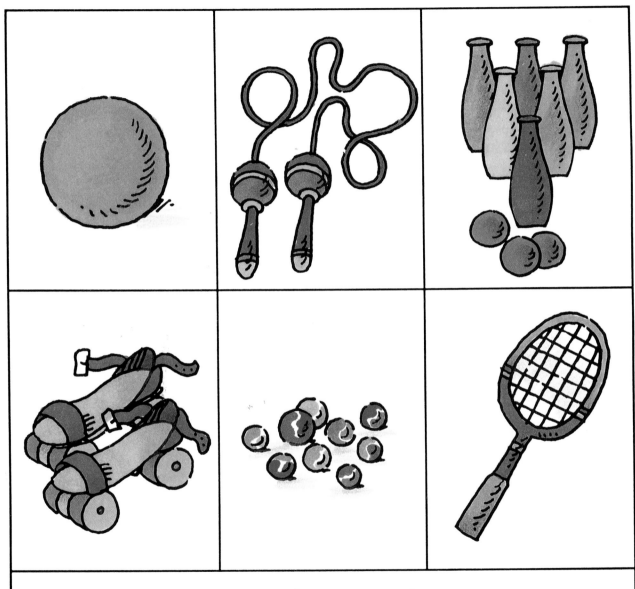

Can you say what games these are?

3 o'clock
Off to the shops with mother.
How is Ted helping his mother?

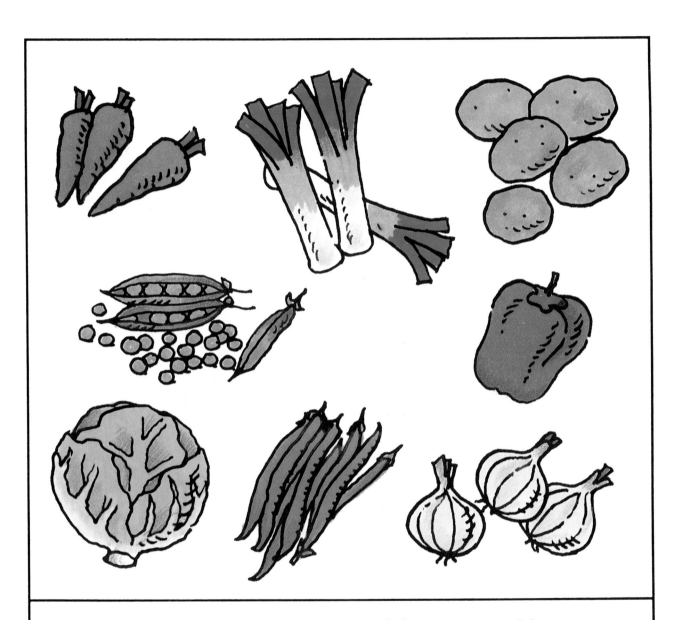

Do you know the names of these vegetables?

4 o'clock
Television time.
What is your favourite T.V. programme?

Which one does not say 4 o'clock?

5 o'clock
A picnic in the garden.
What does Ted like to drink?

Which ant has collected the most crumbs?

6 o'clock
Time for a bath.
Can you blow bubbles?

7 o'clock
Ted is tucked up in bed.
Is he asleep yet?

Twelve different clocks.

Can you say the time on each one?

We hope you
enjoyed learning
about
TIME

Caroline and John Astrop live by the sea.
They work together on both
illustrations and text for their books.
Surrounded by a large family with children
of all ages, a rich source of ideas and
inspiration, their books are based on the
simple theme that little ones learn more
easily when they are having fun.